INSIDE THE
NFL

# HOUSTON
# TEXANS

*BY TODD RYAN*

SportsZone

An Imprint of Abdo Publishing
abdobooks.com

**abdobooks.com**

Published by Abdo Publishing, a division of ABDO, PO Box 398166, Minneapolis, Minnesota 55439. Copyright © 2020 by Abdo Consulting Group, Inc. International copyrights reserved in all countries. No part of this book may be reproduced in any form without written permission from the publisher. SportsZone™ is a trademark and logo of Abdo Publishing.

Printed in the United States of America, North Mankato, Minnesota
022019
092019

THIS BOOK CONTAINS
RECYCLED MATERIALS

Cover Photo: Aaron M. Sprecher/AP Images
Interior Photos: Dave Einsel/AP Images, 5; Smiley N. Pool/Houston Chronicle/AP Images, 7; Tony Gutierrez/AP Images, 11, 31; Pat Sullivan/AP Images, 13; Photo File/AP Images, 15, 43; Steve Mitchell/AP Images, 17; Mark Lennihan/AP Images, 19; David J. Phillip/AP Images, 21; Brett Coomer/AP Images, 22, 25; Paul Spinelli/AP Images, 27; G. Newman Lowrance/AP Images, 29, 41; Dave Einsel/AP Images, 33; Bill Baptist/AP Images, 37

Editor: Patrick Donnelly
Series Designer: Craig Hinton

**Library of Congress Control Number: 2018965345**

**Publisher's Cataloging-in-Publication Data**

Names: Ryan, Todd, author.
Title: Houston Texans / by Todd Ryan
Description: Minneapolis, Minnesota: Abdo Publishing, 2020 | Series: Inside the NFL
    | Includes online resources and index.
Identifiers: ISBN 9781532118487 (lib. bdg.) | ISBN 9781532172663 (ebook)
    | ISBN 9781644941072 (pbk.)
Subjects: LCSH: Houston Texans (Football team)--Juvenile literature. | National
    Football League --Juvenile literature. | Football teams--Juvenile literature.
    | American football--Juvenile literature.
Classification: DDC 796.33264--dc23

# TABLE OF
# CONTENTS

# CHAPTER 1

# WINNERS AT LAST

The Houston Texans made their debut as an expansion team in the National Football League (NFL) in 2002. Nine years later, they still had never made the playoffs. They had come close in previous seasons. But when the 2011 season began, Houston and its fans knew the Texans were capable of finally breaking through.

The Texans went 7–3 in their first 10 games that season. It looked as if Houston would not only make the playoffs but be a team that could contend for the American Football Conference (AFC) title.

Defense played a key role in the Texans' success. They had hired a new defensive coordinator before the season. Wade Phillips came in and had Houston playing aggressively.

Arian Foster was a big part of the Texans' first playoff push.

Led by linebacker Brian Cushing and defensive end J. J. Watt, the Texans were getting consistent pressure on the quarterback and forcing a lot of turnovers.

Houston also was clicking on offense. The Texans scored at least 23 points in seven of their first 10 games. But they ran into trouble in Week 10. In a game against the Tampa Bay Buccaneers, starting quarterback Matt Schaub suffered a season-ending foot injury. That meant backup quarterback Matt Leinart would be the next man up, trying to save the Texans' season.

But the bad news kept coming. In Houston's next game, Leinart broke his collarbone and was out for the season. That put rookie third-string quarterback T. J. Yates in the spotlight. Yates was the Texans' fifth-round pick in the 2011 NFL Draft.

Yates came in and was great. He finished off a 20–13 victory over Jacksonville, then started in

## GETTING BETTER

The Texans made steady improvement under head coach Gary Kubiak. In 2006, his first year as coach, Houston went 6–10. This was four wins better than the team's 2005 record. In 2007 the Texans reached 8–8 for the first time. They then went 8–8 again in 2008 before they finally broke .500 by going 9–7 in 2009. Kubiak's teams finished above .500 three times in his eight years in Houston.

✗ Kevin Walter (83) catches the game-winning touchdown pass while T. J. Yates (13) celebrates in the background as the Texans beat the Bengals to clinch the division title.

a 17–10 win against the Atlanta Falcons. In Week 14, Houston rallied from a 19–10 deficit in the fourth quarter. Yates and wide receiver Kevin Walter teamed up on a 6-yard touchdown pass with two seconds to play to pull out a 20–19 victory at Cincinnati. The victory gave the Texans the AFC South division title. They were headed to the playoffs for the first time ever.

## ANDRE JOHNSON

Wide receiver Andre Johnson was one of the Texans' original stars. He was selected with the third pick of the 2003 NFL Draft. Johnson stuck with the Texans through their early struggles. He led the NFL in receiving yards in 2008 and 2009. He only played seven games in 2011 because of injury but was key to the Texans knocking off the Bengals in the team's first playoff victory. Johnson spent 12 seasons in Houston before finishing his career by playing one season in Indianapolis and one season in Tennessee.

The Texans lost their last three regular-season games, but it didn't matter much. They earned the third seed in the AFC playoffs and got to host their first playoff game. More than 70,000 Texans fans filled Reliant Stadium to cheer on their hometown team. And for the second time in a month, Houston and Yates would be playing the Bengals.

The fans roared inside the stadium, but the Bengals scored first to momentarily quiet the crowd. The Texans responded quickly. Though Yates was inexperienced, he had a lot of good players around him. Tight end Owen Daniels and wide receiver Andre Johnson were tough to defend. Arian Foster had developed into a Pro Bowl running back after not even being drafted.

Daniels caught a long pass down the middle, and a penalty tacked onto the play put the ball at the Cincinnati 20-yard line.

## J. J. WATT

Texans defensive end J. J. Watt wasn't always a defensive star. When he started college at Central Michigan University, Watt thought he would be a tight end. But he soon changed his mind. He transferred to the University of Wisconsin and became a fearsome pass rusher. Houston took Watt in the first round of the 2011 draft and he had an immediate impact with 5.5 sacks and two fumble recoveries as a rookie. Watt followed that up with a combined 69.0 sacks over his next four seasons, leading the NFL in 2012 and 2015.

But Watt also had an impact in the community. The city of Houston was devastated by Hurricane Harvey in 2017. The storm damaged thousands of homes in the area. Watt raised more than $40 million to help those affected by the storm. The effort earned Watt *Sports Illustrated's* Sportsperson of the Year award, which he shared with local baseball star Jose Altuve of the Houston Astros.

Foster did the rest, with runs of 8, 4, and 8 yards to score the game-tying touchdown.

The teams traded field goals in the second quarter before the Houston defense made the play of the game. With less than a minute remaining in the first half, Watt intercepted a pass and returned it 29 yards for a touchdown. Houston had scored to take the lead and had the home fans rocking again.

The Texans defense put the clamps on the Bengals from there, intercepting quarterback Andy Dalton two more times. Houston's offense took care of the rest. Yates threw a 40-yard touchdown pass to Johnson to extend the Texans' lead. In the fourth quarter, Foster scored on a 42-yard run. The final score was 31–10. Houston's fans got to celebrate a perfect playoff debut.

The Texans had to travel to Baltimore the following week in the divisional round of the playoffs. It would be tough for any team to beat the Ravens' imposing defense with a rookie quarterback, and the Texans ended up losing 20–13. But it was a strong effort from Houston.

Houston football fans had waited patiently for the NFL to return to the city, ever since the Houston Oilers moved to Tennessee in 1997. They waited even longer for their new team to become a playoff contender. But the faithful supporters who packed Reliant Stadium throughout the 2011 season had to believe their patience had been rewarded.

✗ J. J. Watt celebrates his game-changing touchdown just before halftime in the January 2012 playoff game against Cincinnati.

# CHAPTER 2

# FOOTBALL RETURNS TO HOUSTON

On October 6, 1999, the city of Houston rejoiced. After suffering through the departure of the Houston Oilers for Tennessee in 1996, the NFL was coming back. The league had approved Houston businessman Bob McNair's $700 million bid for an expansion team.

The new team would begin play in 2002. McNair and the city of Houston beat out Los Angeles to receive the league's thirty-second franchise.

"It's an awful lot of money," McNair said after the vote by the league's owners. "But we've got a tremendous product in NFL football, and a stadium that'll knock your socks off."

The road to landing a new team was not a smooth one for McNair. He had started his quest to get an NFL team

Texans owner Bob McNair shows off the new team's logo in 2000. McNair bought the expansion team in 1999.

## TEXANS, PART 5

When Houston owner Bob McNair unveiled the team nickname of the Texans, it was not the first time a professional football team had that name. In 1952 an NFL team called the Dallas Texans played for one year. From 1960 to 1962, Dallas again was the home of a team called the Texans. That team played in the American Football League before moving to Kansas City and becoming the Chiefs. In 1974 Houston was home to a team called the Texans that played in the World Football League. Finally, the San Antonio Texans played in the Canadian Football League in 1995.

back in Houston only months after the Oilers moved to Nashville. Hindering McNair and the city was the fact that the NFL had made it well known that it wanted a team in Los Angeles, the second-largest city in the United States but an NFL wasteland since 1995, when the Rams and Raiders skipped town. But Houston, the nation's fourth-largest city, had a stadium plan in place and an owner who was committed to keeping the team in the city.

Still, in March 1999, the NFL Expansion Committee voted 29–2 to give Los Angeles six months to work out a stadium plan and find an ownership group. In the end, the league was not satisfied with any of the Los Angeles proposals. Houston was awarded the team instead. "On balance," said Paul Tagliabue, the NFL commissioner at the time, "Houston was superior."

For three years, football fans had been waiting for the return of the NFL. Thanks to McNair, those fans got their wish.

✕ Reliant Stadium was the NFL's first stadium with a retractable roof. Construction began in early 2000, and the facility opened in 2002.

But being awarded a team was just the start of a three-year process to turn the idea of a team into players on a field. The first step was taken on January 19, 2000, when Charley Casserly was hired as the executive vice president and general manager. Casserly was placed in charge of hiring front office executives and a head coach for the team. Up next: a name.

By February 2000, thousands of ideas for possible team names had been narrowed to five: Apollos, Bobcats, Stallions, Texans, and Wildcatters. Bobcats and Wildcatters were the first names to be dropped from the list of finalists. With the help of fans voting online, the official team name of Texans was unveiled in front of thousands of fans at a downtown rally on September 6, 2000. This happened as construction of the NFL's first retractable-roof stadium got underway. The new stadium is located right next to the famed Astrodome, where the Oilers played.

## CEREMONIAL FIRST . . . PASS?

After unveiling the team's name, logo, and colors on September 6, 2000, Texans owner Bob McNair threw the first pitch that night before the Houston Astros of Major League Baseball played host to the Florida Marlins. However, instead of throwing a baseball to Astros owner Drayton McLane, McNair threw a football.

The Texans named Dom Capers the team's first head coach on January 21, 2001. Capers was selected because of his experience in building teams from scratch. He had been the head coach of the expansion Carolina Panthers from 1995 to 1998. He even guided the Panthers to the conference championship game in their second year in the league. The Texans now had a nickname and logo.

✖ Dom Capers, shown in 2003, was hired as the Texans' head coach in 2001.

A state-of-the-art stadium was being built. Team colors had been chosen. A head coach had been hired. But they still had no players.

The team held workouts for free agents at the Astrodome. A few players were signed. Then the NFL held an expansion draft in February 2002. The Texans were allowed to choose from a group of players made available by other NFL teams. Five-time Pro Bowl player Tony Boselli, an offensive tackle with the Jacksonville Jaguars, was Houston's first pick.

## CARR GIVEN FRANCHISE KEYS

When David Carr was selected with the first pick in the 2002 NFL Draft, he made history in a couple of different ways. He was the first-ever college draft choice of the Texans. He was also the first Fresno State athlete to be a number one selection in any sport.

Carr was coming off a standout senior season. He had won the Johnny Unitas Golden Arm Award and the Sammy Baugh Trophy after leading the nation in passing yards (4,308) and touchdowns (42). Carr was only the sixth major-college quarterback ever to pass for 4,000 yards and 40 touchdowns in a season.

"We have a Hall of Famer, and we haven't played a game," Casserly said.

Unfortunately for the Texans, Boselli had to retire due to multiple injuries before he ever played a game for Houston. However, the Texans had better luck with the 18 other players they selected. Offensive tackle Ryan Young, cornerbacks Aaron Glenn and Marcus Coleman, defensive tackles Gary Walker and Seth Payne, and linebacker Jamie Sharper all became important players for Houston.

Two months later, the Texans chose David Carr from Fresno State with the first selection in the NFL Draft. The Texans selected 11 other players in that 2002 college draft. But it was Carr who quickly became the face of the team. He signed a contract with the club on the day of the draft. His play in the coming years would be a big factor in whether the

David Carr and his mother, Sheryl, embrace after the Texans selected him with the first overall pick in the 2002 NFL Draft.

Texans succeeded or experienced the struggles typical of an expansion team.

# CHAPTER 3

# UPS AND DOWNS

When the schedule for the Texans' first season came out, the team's first regular-season game stood out above the rest. It was a Sunday night game on national TV against the Dallas Cowboys, a team despised by many Houston football fans.

"This game goes way beyond Cal-Stanford levels, and that's saying a lot," said Texans linebacker Kailee Wong, who played for Stanford University in its annual rivalry game against the University of California. "But that's kind of what this game feels like here. It's kind of like in college, where you have that one big game, and it doesn't matter how you do for the rest of the season, as long as you win the game."

The sellout crowd of 69,604 at Houston's new facility, Reliant Stadium, was roaring long before the game against the Cowboys started on September 8, 2002.

Quarterback David Carr is pumped up for the Texans' first regular-season game on September 8, 2002.

✕ Texans cornerback Aaron Glenn celebrates an interception during Houston's win over Dallas to open the 2002 season.

On the field, Houston quickly showed that it was ready to compete in the NFL. On the first play from scrimmage in Texans history, David Carr threw a deep pass to wide receiver

Corey Bradford. The pass was incomplete. But pass interference was called. That moved Houston 43 yards to the Dallas 21-yard line.

Three plays later, Texans fans went delirious when tight end Billy Miller hauled in a 19-yard pass from Carr for the first touchdown in team history. The Texans then built a 10–0 lead in the second quarter on Kris Brown's 42-yard field goal.

Dallas came back and tied the score midway through the third quarter. But Houston scored on a 65-yard pass from Carr to Bradford on the opening drive of the fourth quarter. Nose tackle Seth Payne then sacked Cowboys quarterback Quincy Carter in the end zone for a safety with 2:37 remaining to give the Texans a 19–10 lead. They held on to win by that score.

The excitement did not translate into many more victories, however. Houston lost its next five games before it defeated Jacksonville 21–19 on a late field goal by Brown. The win was the Texans' first in

## MAKING HISTORY

Cornerback Aaron Glenn and defensive end Gary Walker were selected to play in the Pro Bowl in 2002. Houston was the first first-year expansion team to have representatives at the Pro Bowl since the New Orleans Saints in 1967, when all teams had to have at least one player selected.

a road game. Houston won only two more games the rest of the season to finish 4–12. One victory came against the Pittsburgh Steelers. The Texans won 24–6 despite not scoring an offensive touchdown. Cornerback Aaron Glenn returned two interceptions for touchdowns and the defense forced five turnovers.

With the Texans' arrival in 2002, the NFL created four divisions in each of its two conferences. Previously, each conference had three divisions. Joining Houston in the AFC South were the Indianapolis Colts, Jacksonville Jaguars, and Tennessee Titans. The Texans would play each of those teams twice a season.

In its first season, Houston finished last in the South. But with that season in the books, the Texans were looking forward to 2003. They believed that they would be an improved team. Carr would have a full season of experience. In addition, dynamic wide receiver Andre Johnson arrived via the draft to add a future Pro Bowl talent to Carr's targets.

The Texans again won their season opener, defeating the Miami Dolphins 21–20 on the road. Through its first 12 games, Houston was 5–7. But the Texans then lost their final four games to finish 5–11. While the Texans did not do as well

✗ Houston's Andre Johnson, *right*, battles New England's Tyrone Poole in 2003. Johnson finished his rookie season with 976 receiving yards.

as they hoped for on the field, Johnson and running back Domanick Davis had outstanding rookie seasons. Johnson, the team's first-round draft choice out of the University of Miami, had 66 receptions for 976 yards and four touchdowns. Davis, a former Louisiana State University standout drafted in the fourth round, became the first player in league history to win NFL Rookie of the Week honors four straight times.

## DOMANICK DAVIS

Domanick Davis burst onto the NFL scene in 2003 by rushing for 1,031 yards and eight touchdowns. The performance was good enough for him to be named the NFL Rookie of the Year. Davis was even better in 2004. He rushed for a club-record 1,188 yards and 13 touchdowns. He added 588 receiving yards on 68 receptions.

In 2005, Davis ran for 976 yards in 11 games. But he suffered a knee injury that required surgery. He reported to training camp in 2006 and said he was healthy. But he soon experienced swelling in his knee and needed more surgery. Davis had to miss the entire season. In March 2007, the Texans released him, and he never played in the NFL again.

In 2004 the Texans went 7–9, giving fans hope that the team was about to turn the corner. Carr had his best NFL season. He threw for a career-high 3,531 yards and 16 touchdowns. Johnson had 79 receptions for 1,142 yards and six touchdowns. Davis rushed for 1,188 yards and 13 touchdowns.

But any hopes of a successful season in 2005 were dashed early in the year. The Texans lost their first six games before beating Cleveland 19–16. Another six-game losing streak followed before Houston defeated Arizona 30–19. The Texans finished the season with two more losses, including a 20–17 defeat to San Francisco in the season finale. Houston finished

✘ Texans running back Domanick Davis runs against the Chiefs in 2004.

with a league-worst 2–14 record. Not long after the final game, owner Bob McNair fired Dom Capers, the only head coach the Texans had known.

"I think that we've underachieved this season," McNair said. "I think that everyone expected us to do more."

# CHAPTER 4

# START OF A NEW DIRECTION

Finishing 2–14 in 2005 forced the Texans to start over in 2006. Longtime Denver Broncos offensive coordinator Gary Kubiak was hired as the team's new head coach. One of his first decisions was whom to take with the first selection in the 2006 NFL Draft.

Heisman Trophy–winning running back Reggie Bush of the University of Southern California (USC) was available. So was quarterback Vince Young. Young had grown up in Houston and had guided the University of Texas to the national title. His Texas team beat Bush and USC in the national championship game. But, to the surprise of many, the Texans selected defensive end Mario Williams of North Carolina State.

Mario Williams helped beef up the defense after the Texans chose him with the first pick in the 2006 NFL Draft.

## NEEDING MORE OFFENSE

One of the main reasons the Texans hired Gary Kubiak to become the team's second head coach was his background. Kubiak grew up in Houston, attending St. Pius X High School. He went on to star at Texas A&M University, where he played quarterback. In the NFL, he served as a backup to star John Elway with the Denver Broncos from 1983 to 1991. After a brief coaching stint at A&M, he joined George Seifert's staff with the San Francisco 49ers in 1994. Kubiak served as the quarterbacks coach for one year and earned a Super Bowl ring. He then went to Denver when former San Francisco assistant Mike Shanahan was named the Broncos' coach. Kubiak served as the Broncos' offensive coordinator for 11 seasons, winning two more Super Bowls in the process, before taking over as head coach in Houston.

The move was not very popular with the fans in Houston, who wanted either of the big-name offensive players. But Kubiak believed that he could help quarterback David Carr improve, and that the team's biggest need was for a defensive player such as Williams who could put pressure on opposing quarterbacks.

With Williams now anchoring the defensive line, the defense as a whole played better in 2006. The offense showed some improvement as well. The Texans improved by four wins, finishing 6–10. But another draft pick had an even

Houston linebacker DeMeco Ryans wraps up Dallas running back Julius Jones in 2006. Ryans made an immediate impact for the Texans as a rookie.

bigger impact than Williams. Linebacker DeMeco Ryans was the Texans' second-round pick in 2006. Ryans was a former University of Alabama standout. He made 155 tackles in his first year and was named the NFL Rookie of the Year.

## PROVING HIS VALUE

Mario Williams was not a popular choice among Texans fans when the team chose him with the first pick of the 2006 draft. The 6-foot-6, 295-pound defensive end had a lot to prove. He struggled in his first year with the team, managing only 4.5 sacks. But in 2007, he showed why the Texans wanted him to anchor the defensive line. He made 59 tackles in his second season and, more importantly, added 14.0 sacks. He followed that season with 53 tackles, 12.0 sacks, and his first Pro Bowl appearance in 2008. He came through with 43 tackles and nine sacks and went back to the Pro Bowl in 2009.

On offense, Andre Johnson had his best year yet with 103 receptions for 1,147 yards and five touchdowns. Rookie tight end Owen Daniels added 34 catches for 352 yards and five touchdowns.

However, the expected improvement from Carr did not happen. Although he started all 16 games, Carr passed for only 2,767 yards and 11 touchdowns with 12 interceptions. After the season, the Texans released Carr and worked out a trade with the Atlanta Falcons for quarterback Matt Schaub.

A former third-round pick, Schaub was a backup with Atlanta from 2004 to 2006. He had not played much, but the Texans liked what they saw of him. They believed that he could be a good starting quarterback in the NFL if he were given the chance.

✗ Quarterback Matt Schaub celebrates his 3-yard touchdown run that allowed host Houston to beat Miami 29–28 in October 2008.

The Texans showed their faith in Schaub when they gave him a six-year, $48 million contract. It was the beginning of a new era in Houston. The trio of Schaub, Johnson, and Daniels was expected to help carry the Texans to new heights. Daniels improved in 2007, making 63 catches for 768 yards. But Johnson and Schaub missed a combined 12 games due to injuries. Despite having two of their top offensive players out for part of the season, the Texans won a team-record eight games. Williams led the way on defense with 14.0 sacks. Houston avoided finishing with a losing record for the first time in team history.

The team had high hopes in 2008. But the season was dramatically altered in the early morning hours of September 13. That's when Hurricane Ike made landfall near Galveston Bay and roared right through Houston. The storm damaged the roof at Reliant Stadium. The Texans had lost their season-opening game, 38–17 at Pittsburgh on September 7. Houston's second game of the season was scheduled to be played on September 14 at home against Baltimore. It had to be postponed until November 9 because of the hurricane. As a result, the Texans wound up playing three road games to start the season.

In the two weeks after the hurricane, Houston lost to Tennessee and then to Jacksonville. The Texans finally came home to play Indianapolis at Reliant Stadium on October 5. Houston led 27–10 late in the game. But the Colts scored 21 points in the final four minutes to pull out the victory and stun the Texans 31–27.

Houston was resilient. The team regrouped and defeated visiting Miami 29–28 the next week. Then came victories over the Detroit Lions and the Cincinnati Bengals. The up-and-down play of the team would be its theme in 2008. The three-game winning streak was followed by a three-game losing skid. But then the Texans won four straight games to improve to 7–7. The Texans finished 8–8 for the second consecutive season.

The Texans were expected to contend for a playoff spot in 2009. They did not disappoint. They finished 9–7 but missed the postseason on a tiebreaker. They took a step back in 2010. The Texans started 4–2 and looked like they were on their way to their first playoff appearance. But the team lost eight of its next 10 games to finish 6–10. After feeling hopeful in 2009, Houston fans hoped the 2010 season was just a temporary setback. With most of the same pieces coming back in 2011, the Texans were ready to make that jump into the playoffs.

## BREAKOUT PERFORMANCE

Quarterback Matt Schaub started all 16 games in 2009, even though he suffered a separated left shoulder during the season. Schaub earned a spot in the Pro Bowl after throwing for a league-leading 4,770 yards and 29 touchdowns.

# CHAPTER 5

# TURNING THE CORNER

The Texans relied on an improved defense to carry them to their first playoff appearance in 2011. They fell one game short of the AFC Championship Game, but as they headed into the 2012 season, the Texans knew they could compete in the AFC.

They picked up right where they left off in 2011. The Texans won 11 of their first 12 games in 2012. Matt Schaub was back and healthy after a season-ending injury in 2011. He led a dominant Houston offense that featured a strong running game with Arian Foster and great pass catchers in Andre Johnson and Owen Daniels. The Texans finished 12–4 and won their second straight AFC South title.

Andre Johnson was one of the NFL's top receivers for more than a decade.

Once again, the Texans found themselves hosting Cincinnati in the first round of the playoffs. And once again, the defense came through as Houston won 19–13. Next, the Texans headed on the road to face the powerhouse New England Patriots. The Houston defense struggled against quarterback Tom Brady and the New England offense as the Texans lost 41–28.

Houston followed up two years of playoff berths with two seasons of struggles. Kubiak was fired in 2013 as the Texans went 2–14. Schaub was also out of Houston at this point.

The Texans went with another offense-minded head coach when they hired Bill O'Brien in 2014. He had been the head coach at Penn State University and an offensive assistant with the Patriots.

Despite Houston's recent struggles, O'Brien took over a team that had its share of bright spots. Foster continued to be an effective running back while the Texans had added an exciting young wide receiver in DeAndre Hopkins. He and Johnson both had the ability to amaze fans with their acrobatic catches. Meanwhile, J. J. Watt had emerged as a feared pass rusher to lead the Texans defense.

The Texans went 9–7 in each of O'Brien's first two seasons. In 2015, that record was good enough to win the AFC South.

Watt led a strong defense with 17.5 sacks that season. But in the first round of the AFC playoffs, the Texans were blown out at home 30–0 by the Kansas City Chiefs.

Houston went back to the playoffs in 2016 and won the team's fourth division title. The Texans hosted the Oakland Raiders, who were without starting quarterback Derek Carr, the younger brother of former Texans quarterback David Carr. Houston and its strong defense got past Oakland 27–14, putting the Texans in the divisional round for the third time in six seasons. However, Houston ended up falling short of the AFC Championship Game once again as the Texans lost to New England.

The Texans needed more help to get over the hump and get out of the second round of the playoffs. So they used their first-round pick on a quarterback for the first time since selecting David Carr back in 2002. They went with Deshaun Watson, who had just won a national championship at

## ARIAN FOSTER

Arian Foster signed with the Texans as an undrafted free agent in 2009. But before the season, he was cut and placed on Houston's practice squad. Foster continued to work hard and was activated for six games in 2009. The next year, he became a star as he ran for 1,616 yards and 16 touchdowns with Houston. He ended his eight-year career in 2016 with 54 touchdowns and four Pro Bowl berths.

## DEANDRE HOPKINS

Andre Johnson had solidified himself as the No. 1 receiver in Houston a decade before DeAndre Hopkins joined the Texans in 2013. But Johnson was getting older and Houston needed another receiver who could be the focus of the offense. That ended up being Hopkins. Like Johnson, Hopkins wowed fans with his ability to make acrobatic catches. He and Johnson made for a strong duo for two seasons before Johnson left for Indianapolis in 2015. Hopkins thrived on his own and was named First-Team All-Pro in 2017 and 2018.

Clemson University. Watson started strong and gave fans hope with some outstanding performances, including a 402-yard, four-touchdown effort against the Seattle Seahawks in October. However, a knee injury ended his rookie season early and the Texans went on to finish 4–12.

But Watson bounced back with a strong second season, throwing 26 touchdown passes and rushing for five more scores. Running backs Lamar Miller and Alfred Blue provided a solid one-two punch in the ground game. Hopkins was electric all season, catching 115 passes for 1,572 yards and 11 touchdowns. Watt led the AFC with 16.0 sacks, while fellow

✕ Acrobatic wide receiver DeAndre Hopkins began tormenting NFL defensive backs when he arrived in Houston in 2013.

defensive end Jadeveon Clowney finished with 9.0 sacks and earned his third straight trip to the Pro Bowl.

Houston finished 11–5 and won its third AFC South title in four seasons. The season ended in disappointment, however, as the offense sputtered in a 21–7 loss to the Colts in the first round of the playoffs. But with Watson and Hopkins leading a rejuvenated offense, along with Watt and Clowney providing the backbone to a strong defense, the future looked bright in Houston.

# TIMELINE

On October 6 the NFL awards Houston an expansion franchise to begin play in 2002.

The team's nickname, logo, and colors are officially revealed on September 6.

The Texans add 19 players to their roster in the NFL Expansion Draft on February 18.

On April 20, the Texans select quarterback David Carr of Fresno State as their first-ever choice in the NFL Draft.

Houston wins its first NFL game when it stuns the visiting Dallas Cowboys 19–10 in the season opener on September 8.

**1999**

**2000**

**2002**

**2002**

**2002**

Cornerback Aaron Glenn and defensive end Gary Walker become the first Pro Bowl players in franchise history, starting for the AFC team on February 2.

On April 26 the Texans select wide receiver Andre Johnson of Miami with the third pick in the NFL Draft.

Running back Domanick Davis earns the NFL Rookie of the Year Award.

Johnson, on February 13, becomes the first Texans offensive player to play in the Pro Bowl.

Linebacker DeMeco Ryans becomes the first Texans player to earn NFL Defensive Rookie of the Year honors.

**2003**

**2003**

**2003**

**2005**

**2006**

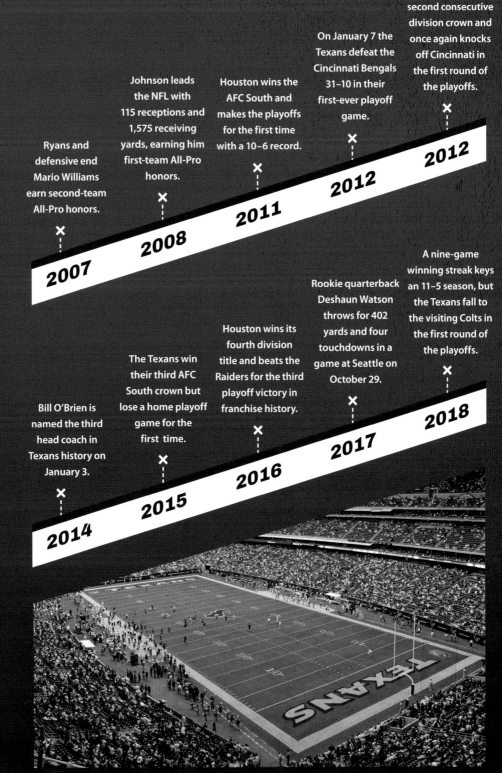

Ryans and defensive end Mario Williams earn second-team All-Pro honors.

✕

**2007**

Johnson leads the NFL with 115 receptions and 1,575 receiving yards, earning him first-team All-Pro honors.

✕

**2008**

Houston wins the AFC South and makes the playoffs for the first time with a 10–6 record.

✕

**2011**

On January 7 the Texans defeat the Cincinnati Bengals 31–10 in their first-ever playoff game.

✕

**2012**

Houston wins its second consecutive division crown and once again knocks off Cincinnati in the first round of the playoffs.

✕

**2012**

Bill O'Brien is named the third head coach in Texans history on January 3.

✕

**2014**

The Texans win their third AFC South crown but lose a home playoff game for the first time.

✕

**2015**

Houston wins its fourth division title and beats the Raiders for the third playoff victory in franchise history.

✕

**2016**

Rookie quarterback Deshaun Watson throws for 402 yards and four touchdowns in a game at Seattle on October 29.

✕

**2017**

A nine-game winning streak keys an 11–5 season, but the Texans fall to the visiting Colts in the first round of the playoffs.

✕

**2018**

# QUICK STATS

## FRANCHISE HISTORY

2002–

## SUPER BOWLS

None

## DIVISION CHAMPIONSHIPS

2011, 2012, 2015, 2016, 2018

## KEY COACHES

Dom Capers (2002–05): 18–46, 0–0 (playoffs)

Gary Kubiak (2006–13): 61–64, 2–2 (playoffs)

Bill O'Brien (2014– ): 42–38, 1–3 (playoffs)

## KEY PLAYERS
### *(position, seasons with team)*

Duane Brown (G, 2008–17)
Kris Brown (K, 2002–09)
David Carr (QB, 2002–06)
Brian Cushing (LB, 2009–17)
Owen Daniels (TE, 2006–13)
Domanick Davis (RB, 2003–05)
Arian Foster (RB, 2009–15)
Aaron Glenn (CB, 2002–04)
Andre Johnson (WR, 2003–14)
Jonathan Joseph (DB, 2011– )
Chris Myers (OG, 2008–14)
Chester Pitts (OL, 2002–09)
Dunta Robinson (CB, 2004–09)
DeMeco Ryans (LB, 2006–11)
Matt Schaub (QB, 2007–13)
Deshaun Watson (QB, 2017– )
J. J. Watt (DE, 2011– )
Mario Williams (DE, 2006–11)
Eric Winston (OT, 2006–11)

## HOME FIELD

NRG Stadium (2002– )
Also known as Reliant Stadium

*All statistics through the 2018 season

# QUOTES AND ANECDOTES

---

*"Now they can go back to Dallas and have a hard-knock life. We ruined their season."*

*—Defensive end Gary Walker, after Houston defeated the Dallas Cowboys in the Texans' first regular-season game in 2002*

---

*"I am retiring because of medical reasons, specifically my left shoulder, which did not continue to improve to the point where I could play. I am disappointed that I will not be able to play for the Texans and do what I was brought here to do."*

*—Offensive tackle Tony Boselli, Houston's first choice in the 2002 NFL Expansion Draft, announcing his retirement in 2003*

---

*"This is another exciting moment in the history of the Texans. . . . Winning is all about getting better every day, and that's what we're trying to do."*

*—Houston owner Bob McNair, after the club traded for and then signed quarterback Matt Schaub to a long-term contract in 2007*

---

Though the Texans were the newest team in the NFL as of 2018, they do have a Ring of Honor. It began in 2017 when standout wide receiver Andre Johnson was inducted.

# GLOSSARY

**All-Pro**
An award given to the top players at their positions, regardless of their conference. It is a high honor as there are fewer spots on the All-Pro team than on the Pro Bowl teams.

**berth**
A place, spot, or position, such as in the NFL playoffs.

**contend**
To compete.

**contract**
An agreement to play for a certain team.

**expansion**
The addition of new teams to increase the size of a league.

**franchise**
A sports organization, including the top-level team and all minor league affiliates.

**Heisman Trophy**
The award given yearly to the best player in college football.

**Pro Bowl**
The NFL's all-star game, in which the best players in the league compete.

**rookie**
A professional athlete in his or her first year of competition.

**sack**
A tackle of the quarterback behind the line of scrimmage before he can pass the ball.

# MORE INFORMATION

## BOOKS

Karras, Steven M. *Houston Texans*. New York: AV2 by Weigl, 2018.

Myers, Dan. *Make Me the Best Football Player*. Minneapolis, MN: Abdo Publishing, 2017.

Norman, J. T. *Houston Texans*. Minneapolis, MN: Abdo Publishing, 2017.

## ONLINE RESOURCES

To learn more about the Houston Texans, visit **abdobooklinks.com** or scan this QR code. These links are routinely monitored and updated to provide the most current information available.

## PLACES TO VISIT

**Houston Methodist Training Center**
8799 Kirby Dr.
Houston, TX 77054
832–667–6000
**houstontexans.com/tickets/training-camp**

This is where the Houston Texans train before each season. Fans have a chance to check out a practice and meet the team mascot.

# INDEX

# ABOUT THE AUTHOR

Todd Ryan is a library assistant from the Upper Peninsula of Michigan. He lives near Houghton with his two cats, Izzo and Mooch.